English Code S
Journey
STARTER
Student's Book

Contents

Unit	Unit aims	Vocabulary	New Language
Welcome! pp. 4–7	**How can I enjoy my first day?** • Learn greetings • Learn number words • Talk about age	hello, goodbye, teacher, girl, boy, good **Numbers:** 1–10	What's your name? I'm … (+ name) How are you? I'm good.
1 Birthday fun! pp. 8–17	**How can I make a birthday card?** • Use birthday and color words. • Talk about birthdays. • Talk about favorite colors.	**Colors:** red, blue, green, yellow, pink, purple, orange, white. **Birthday:** balloon, gift, card, cake, birthday party, candle	It's …, Yes / No, It's a/an (color) (noun)
2 Music time! pp. 18–27	**How can I make a musical instrument?** • Use musical instrument words. • Talk about music. • Talk about musical sounds.	**Music:** drum, shaker, triangle, piano, guitar, trumpet, sing, dance	Let's …
3 At the farm pp. 28–37	**How can I make a toy farm?** • Use farm words. • Talk about farm animals. • Give instructions.	**Farm:** sheep, chicken, cow, duck, tractor, fox, bees, egg	There is / are
Culture 1	**Animals in music**	pp. 38–39	
4 My dinosaur pp. 40–49	**How can I make a dinosaur puzzle?** • Use dinosaur words. • Talk about dinosaurs. • Give support and praise.	**Dinosaurs:** dinosaur, legs, tail, teeth, wings, spines, horn, lizard	It has … It doesn't have …
5 A picnic pp. 50–59	**How can we have a picnic?** • Use picnic words. • Talk about picnics. • Give instructions.	**Food:** pizza, yogurt, fruit, sandwiches, chocolate, tomatoes, milk, salad	I like / don't like
6 Under the sea pp. 60–69	**How can I make a diving game?** • Use sea animal words. • Talk about sea animals. • Talk about the weather.	**Sea animals:** crab, fish, jellyfish, shrimp, shell, starfish, seahorse, shark	Can you see …? Yes, I can. No, I can't.
Culture 2	**Lunch on the go**	pp. 70–71	

Values	Phonics (sound lab)	STEAM	Communication	Project and Review
Be welcoming.			Communication: How old are you? I'm … (+ age)	
Take care of pets.	c, b cake, card, balloon, blue	Science: Rainbows Experiment: How can I make a rainbow?	Communication: What's your favorite color? My favorite color is …	Make a birthday card
Listen to each other.	t, d door, dance, dog, door, table, teacher	Science: Sound waves Experiment: How can I make a water xylophone?	Communication: It's noisy / quiet	Make a musical instrument
Take care of animals.	a, f ant, apple, fox, forest	Science: Food from animals Experiment: How can I make butter?	Communication: Open the (gate / door). / Shut the (gate / door).	Make a toy farm
Give support.	l, e lizard, lunch, leg, egg, elephant, elbow	Science: What dinosaurs eat Experiment: How can I make dinosaur teeth?	Communication: Is it a …? Yes, good job! / No. Nice try!	Make a dinosaur puzzle
Learn to share.	y, j yo-yo, jam, jug, yogurt	Science: Quantities of sugar Experiment: How many spoons of sugar are in my food and drink?	Communication: Wash your hands. / Dry your hands.	Have a picnic
Wear suitable clothes.	i, u insect, igloo, instruments, umbrella, up	Science: Animals with shells Experiment: Can I dissolve a shell?	Communication: It's hot / cold / windy.	Make a diving game

WELCOME!

HOW CAN I ENJOY MY FIRST DAY?

I WILL LEARN GREETINGS.

WELCOME!

HOW OLD ARE YOU?
COMMUNICATION

I WILL LEARN NUMBERS 1–10.

1 LISTEN, POINT, AND CHANT.

VALUES BE WELCOMING.

2 WATCH. HOW OLD ARE THEY?

3 COMPLETE. THEN SAY.

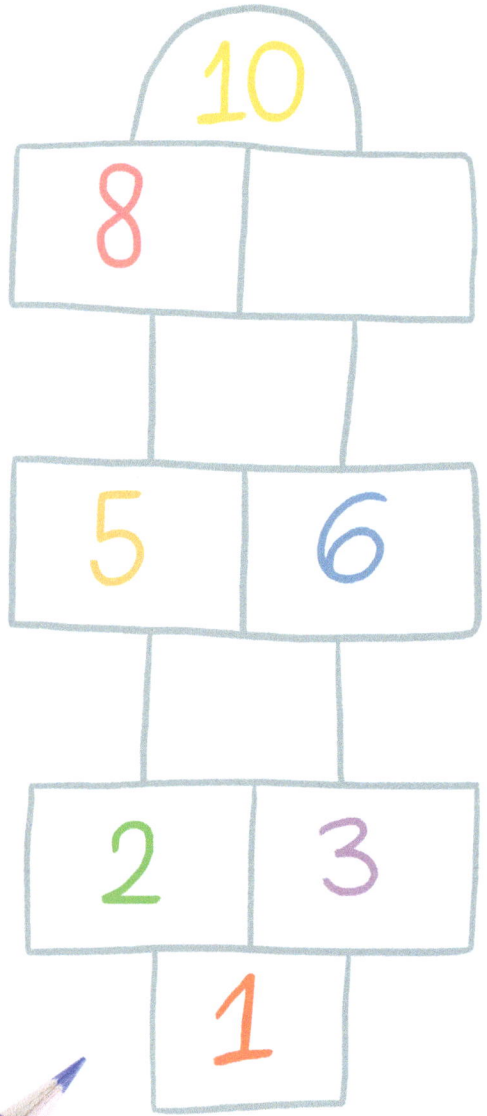

4 PLAY *HOPSCOTCH*.

5 LISTEN AND CIRCLE. THEN ASK AND ANSWER.

8 9 10   4 5 6   7 8 9   1 2 3

6 ASK AND ANSWER. HOW OLD ARE YOU? MAKE A POSTER.

1 BIRTHDAY FUN!
HOW CAN I MAKE A BIRTHDAY CARD?

I WILL LEARN COLORS AND BIRTHDAY WORDS.

1 LOOK AT THE PICTURE. WHAT CAN YOU SEE?

2 STICK THE BIRTHDAY ITEMS ON THE PICTURE.

3 LISTEN, POINT, AND REPEAT.

SONG TIME

4 008 LISTEN AND POINT. THEN SING ALONG AND DANCE.

5 CONTINUE THE SEQUENCE. SAY THE COLORS.

CODE CRACKER

STORY LAB
ENJOYING A STORY

I WILL LISTEN TO A STORY ABOUT A BIRTHDAY.

1 LISTEN TO THE STORY.

HELLO FLUFFY!

VALUES TAKE CARE OF PETS.

2 LOOK AND NUMBER.

3 COLOR THE CAKE AND SAY. THEN DRAW CANDLES.

4 PAINT WITH BUBBLES. DESCRIBE THE COLORS.

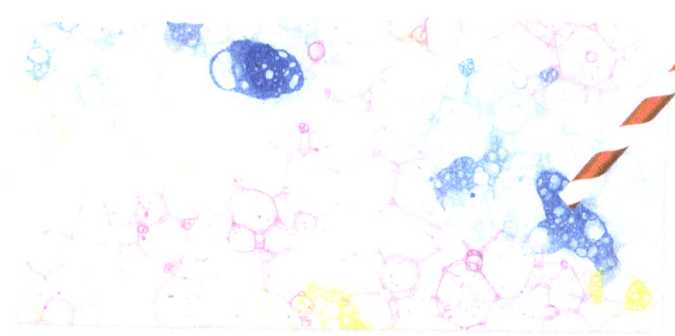

5 ACT OUT THE STORY IN GROUPS.

SOUND LAB
C AND B

> I WILL LEARN THE **C** AND **B** SOUNDS.

1 🎧 010 **LISTEN, POINT, AND REPEAT.**

2 🎧 011 **LISTEN, POINT, AND REPEAT. LISTEN AND FOLLOW. SAY THE SOUNDS.**

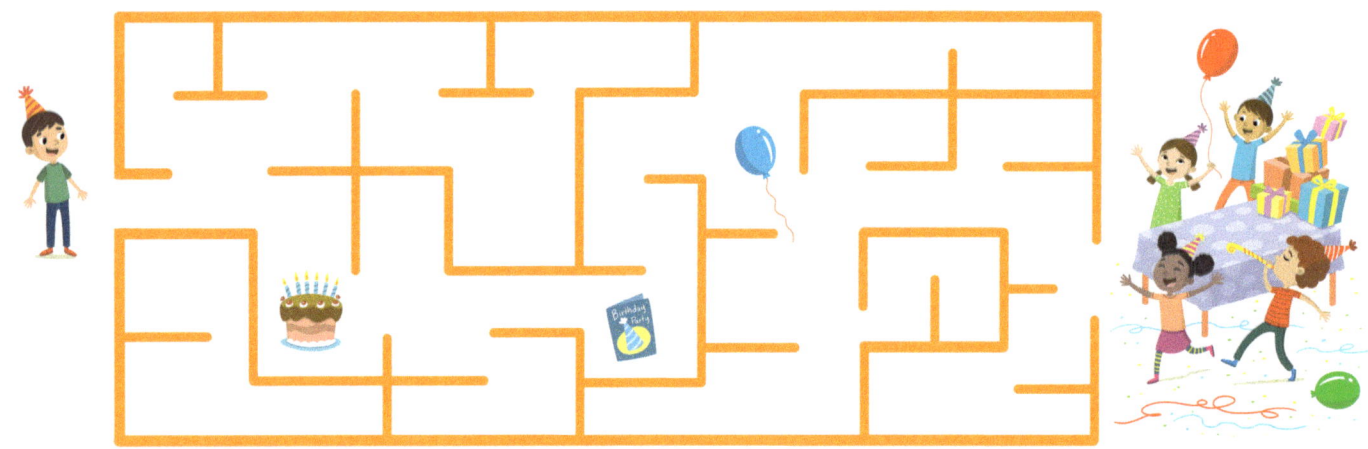

3 💬 **PLAY *BALLOON SOUNDS*.**

4 🎨 **MAKE A CAKE LETTER. SAY THE SOUND.**

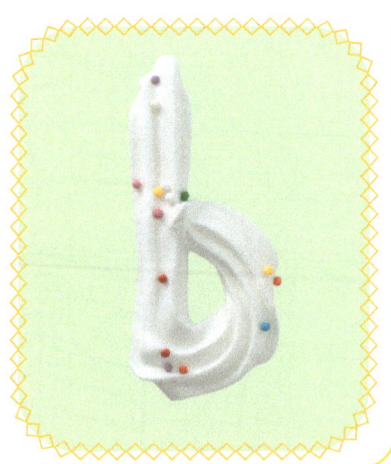

12 TWELVE

EXPERIMENT LAB
SCIENCE: RAINBOWS

I WILL LEARN ABOUT RAINBOWS.

1 LISTEN AND POINT.

WATCH A VIDEO ABOUT RAINBOWS.

2 CHECK ☑ THE THINGS YOU NEED FOR A RAINBOW.

3 LOOK AT THE RAINBOWS IN **1**. SAY THE COLORS WITH YOUR PARTNER.

EXPERIMENT TIME

HOW CAN I MAKE A RAINBOW?

1

2

3

THIRTEEN 13

WHAT'S YOUR FAVORITE COLOR?
COMMUNICATION

I WILL ASK AND ANSWER ABOUT FAVORITE COLORS.

1 COLOR BY NUMBER. THEN SAY.

2 WATCH. COLOR THE BALLOONS.

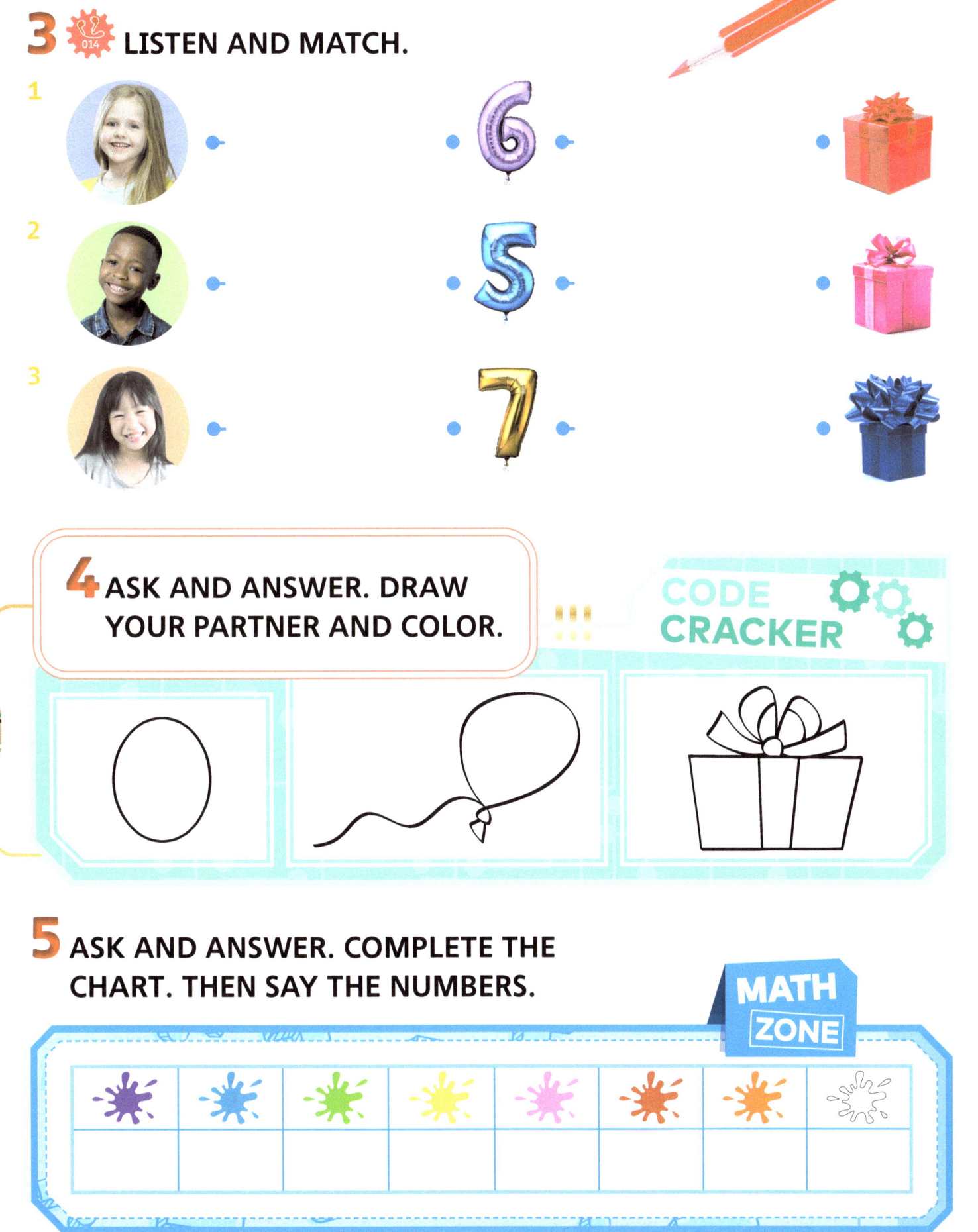

PROJECT AND REVIEW

MAKE A BIRTHDAY CARD

STEP 1

RESEARCH

 RESEARCH FAVORITE COLORS.

☐ WHAT'S MY FRIEND'S FAVORITE COLOR?

STEP 2

PLAN

 CHOOSE COLORS TO USE.

☐ WHICH COLORS CAN I USE?

16 SIXTEEN

STEP 3

CREATE

▷ SCRATCH YOUR CARD.

☐ WHAT CAN I DRAW?

LEARN HOW TO SING *HAPPY BIRTHDAY*.

STEP 4

SHOW AND TELL

▷ ASK AND ANSWER.

NOW I CAN ...

... USE BIRTHDAY AND COLOR WORDS.

... TALK ABOUT BIRTHDAYS.

... TALK ABOUT FAVORITE COLORS.

SEVENTEEN 17

STORY LAB
ENJOYING A STORY

I WILL LISTEN TO A STORY ABOUT MUSIC.

1 LISTEN TO THE STORY.

PLAY THE DRUM, FLUFFY!

2 NUMBER IN ORDER.

CODE CRACKER

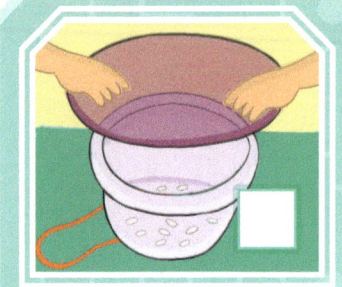

3 🎨 MAKE A MUSIC SPINNER. SPIN, SAY, AND MIME.

4 🎨 ACT OUT THE STORY IN GROUPS. PLAY MUSICAL INSTRUMENTS.

SOUND LAB
T AND D

I WILL LEARN THE **T** AND **D** SOUNDS.

1 LISTEN, POINT, AND REPEAT.

2 LISTEN, POINT, AND REPEAT. MATCH THE WORDS THAT START WITH THE SAME SOUND.

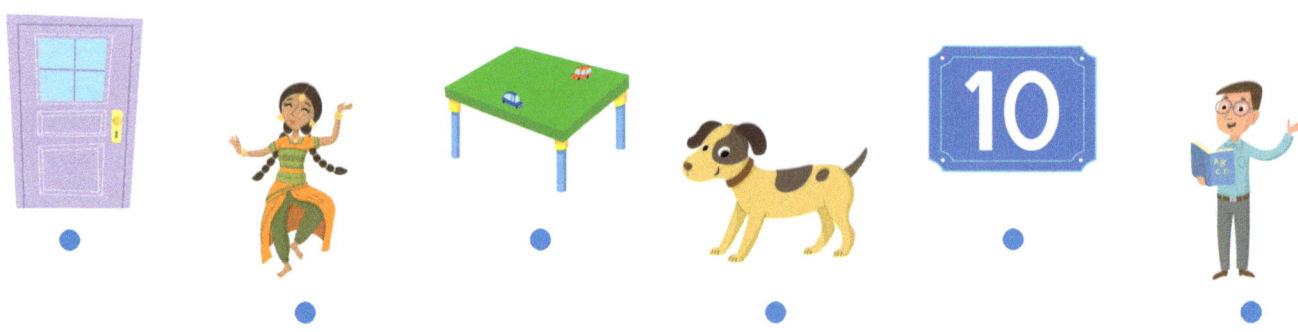

3 PLAY *MUSICAL SCALES*.

4 MAKE LETTER SHAPES IN GROUPS.

EXPERIMENT LAB
SCIENCE: SOUND WAVES

I WILL LEARN ABOUT SOUND WAVES.

▶ WATCH A VIDEO ABOUT SOUND WAVES.

EXPERIMENT TIME

HOW CAN I MAKE A WATER XYLOPHONE?

1 📞 020 LISTEN AND FOLLOW.

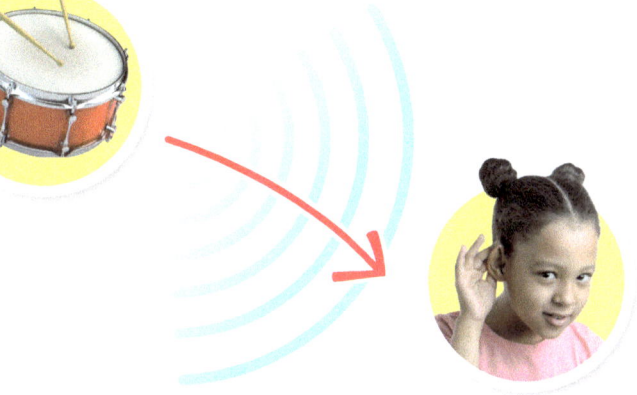

2 📞 021 IS THE SOUND THE SAME? LISTEN AND SAY *YES* OR *NO*.

3 TRACE THE SOUND WAVES.

TWENTY-THREE 23

IT'S NOISY!
COMMUNICATION

I WILL TALK ABOUT MUSICAL SOUNDS.

1 FIND AND DRAW. SAY.

MATH ZONE

2 WATCH. MATCH AND SAY.

3 LISTEN, CHECK ✓, AND SAY.

VALUES: LISTEN TO EACH OTHER.

4 LISTEN AND POINT. DRAW 😃 OR 🙁 AND SAY.

5 PLAY *WHISPERS*.

PROJECT AND REVIEW

MAKE A MUSICAL INSTRUMENT

STEP 1

RESEARCH

- RESEARCH MUSICAL INSTRUMENTS.
- ☐ WHAT MUSICAL INSTRUMENT CAN I MAKE?

STEP 2

PLAN

- DECIDE WHAT MATERIALS YOU NEED.
- ☐ HOW CAN I MAKE MUSICAL INSTRUMENTS?

STEP 3

CREATE

> MAKE YOUR MUSICAL INSTRUMENT.

☐ HOW CAN I DECORATE MY MUSICAL INSTRUMENT?

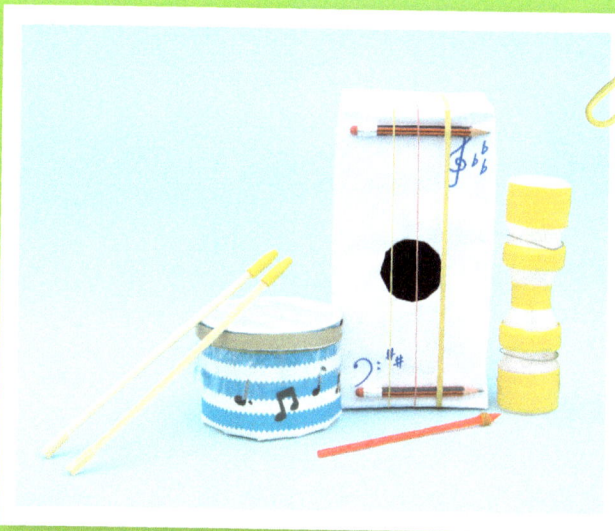

> PERFORM YOUR FAVORITE SONG.

STEP 4

SHOW AND TELL

> PLAY YOUR MUSICAL INSTRUMENT.

NOW I CAN ...

- ... USE MUSICAL INSTRUMENT WORDS.
- ... TALK ABOUT MUSIC.
- ... TALK ABOUT MUSICAL SOUNDS.

TWENTY-SEVEN 27

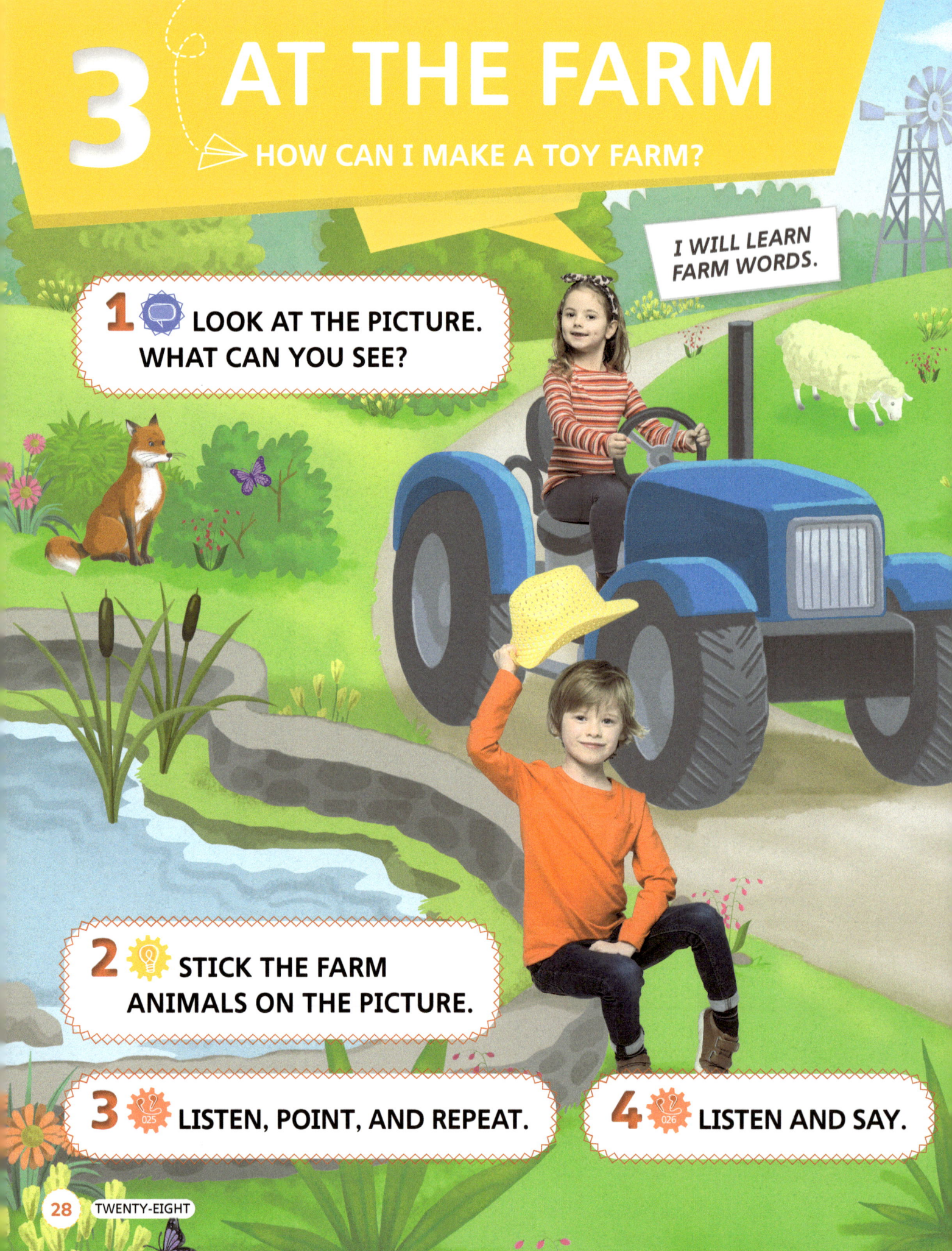

SONG TIME

5 LISTEN AND POINT. THEN SING ALONG AND DANCE.

6 LOOK AND SAY.

STORY LAB
ENJOYING A STORY

I WILL LISTEN TO A STORY ABOUT A FOX.

1 LISTEN TO THE STORY.

THE RED FOX

2 HELP THE FOX FIND ITS CUBS. LOOK AND SAY.

3 🌱 MAKE MARBLED EGGS. DESCRIBE YOUR EGGS.

4 🌱 ACT OUT IN GROUPS. USE YOUR EGGS.

SOUND LAB

> I WILL LEARN THE A AND F SOUNDS.

1 LISTEN, POINT, AND REPEAT.

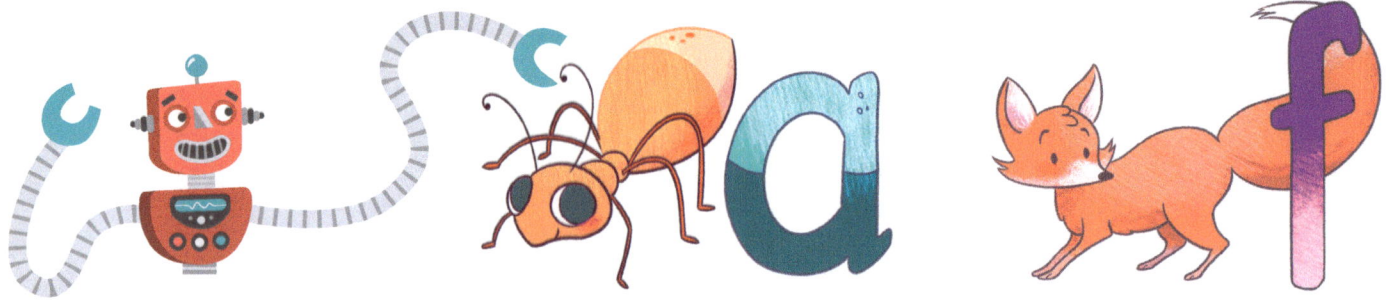

2 LISTEN, POINT, AND REPEAT. FOLLOW THE MAZE AND SAY.

3 SAY THE NUMBERS. CIRCLE THE NUMBERS THAT START WITH F.

4 MAKE LETTERS USING NATURAL MATERIALS. SAY THE SOUND.

EXPERIMENT LAB

SCIENCE: FOOD FROM ANIMALS

I WILL LEARN ABOUT FOOD FROM ANIMALS.

1 🎧 031 **LISTEN AND FOLLOW.**

▶ WATCH A VIDEO ABOUT BEES.

2 NUMBER IN ORDER.

CODE CRACKER

EXPERIMENT TIME

HOW CAN I MAKE BUTTER?

1

2

3

3 💡 **MAKE A COLLAGE ABOUT WHERE FOOD COMES FROM.**

THIRTY-THREE 33

SHUT THE GATE!
COMMUNICATION

I WILL GIVE INSTRUCTIONS.

1 CIRCLE FIVE DIFFERENCES AND SAY.

CODE CRACKER

2 WATCH AND WRITE THE NUMBER. THEN SAY AND MATCH TO A PICTURE IN **1**.

MATH ZONE

VALUES TAKE CARE OF ANIMALS.

3  WATCH AGAIN. DRAW 😀 OR 🙁.

4  LISTEN AND PLAY *TEDDY SAYS*.

5  MAKE AND PLAY *SHUT THE GATE*.

PROJECT AND REVIEW

MAKE A TOY FARM

STEP 1

RESEARCH

- RESEARCH FARM ANIMALS.
- ☐ WHAT ANIMALS CAN YOU SEE AT A FARM?

STEP 2

PLAN

- DECIDE WHERE THE ANIMALS LIVE.
- ☐ WHERE DO THE ANIMALS LIVE?

STEP 3

CREATE

🛪 MAKE YOUR TOY FARM.

☐ WHAT MATERIALS CAN I USE?

FIND OUT ABOUT BABY ANIMALS.

STEP 4

SHOW AND TELL

🛪 TALK ABOUT YOUR TOY FARM.

NOW I CAN ...

... USE FARM WORDS.

... TALK ABOUT FARM ANIMALS.

... GIVE INSTRUCTIONS.

THIRTY-SEVEN 37

CULTURE 1
ANIMALS IN MUSIC

1 🎧 💡 LISTEN AND GUESS THE ANIMALS.

2 🎧 LISTEN AND POINT.

3 🔬 MAKE YOUR OWN CHICKEN IN A CUP MUSICAL INSTRUMENT. PLAY *WHAT'S THAT MUSIC?*

MY CULTURE

FIND OUT ABOUT MUSIC AND ANIMALS IN YOUR COUNTRY.

4 DESCRIBE THE MUSIC TO YOUR PARTNER.

4 MY DINOSAUR
HOW CAN I MAKE A DINOSAUR PUZZLE?

I WILL LEARN DINOSAUR WORDS.

1 LOOK AT THE PICTURE. WHAT CAN YOU SEE?

2 STICK THE DINOSAURS ON THE PICTURE.

3 LISTEN, POINT, AND REPEAT.

SONG TIME

4 LISTEN AND POINT. THEN SING ALONG AND DANCE.

5 COUNT AND SAY.

MATH ZONE

1

2

STORY LAB
ENJOYING A STORY

I WILL LISTEN TO A STORY ABOUT A DINOSAUR.

1 LISTEN TO THE STORY.

IT'S A DINOSAUR!

2 CHECK ✓ OR CROSS ✗ AND SAY.

CODE CRACKER

3 MAKE BINOCULARS. DESCRIBE ANIMALS.

4 ACT OUT THE STORY IN GROUPS. USE YOUR BINOCULARS.

FORTY-THREE 43

SOUND LAB
L AND E

I WILL LEARN THE L AND E SOUNDS.

1 🔊 039 **LISTEN, POINT, AND REPEAT.**

2 🔊 040 **LISTEN, POINT, AND REPEAT. CIRCLE AND SAY THE ODD ONE OUT.**

3 **PLAY THE *RIBBON LETTER SHAPE GAME*.**

4 **MAKE A FOOTPRINT LETTER. SAY THE SOUND.**

EXPERIMENT LAB
SCIENCE: WHAT DINOSAURS EAT

I WILL LEARN ABOUT WHAT DINOSAURS EAT.

1 LISTEN AND POINT.

WATCH A VIDEO ABOUT DINOSAURS.

2 FOLLOW THE MAZE TO THE CORRECT FOOD, AND SAY.

3 COUNT YOUR FLAT AND SHARP TEETH.

EXPERIMENT TIME

HOW CAN I MAKE DINOSAUR TEETH?

1

2

FORTY-FIVE 45

IS IT A DINOSAUR?
COMMUNICATION

I WILL GIVE SUPPORT TO MY FRIENDS.

1 MATCH AND SAY.

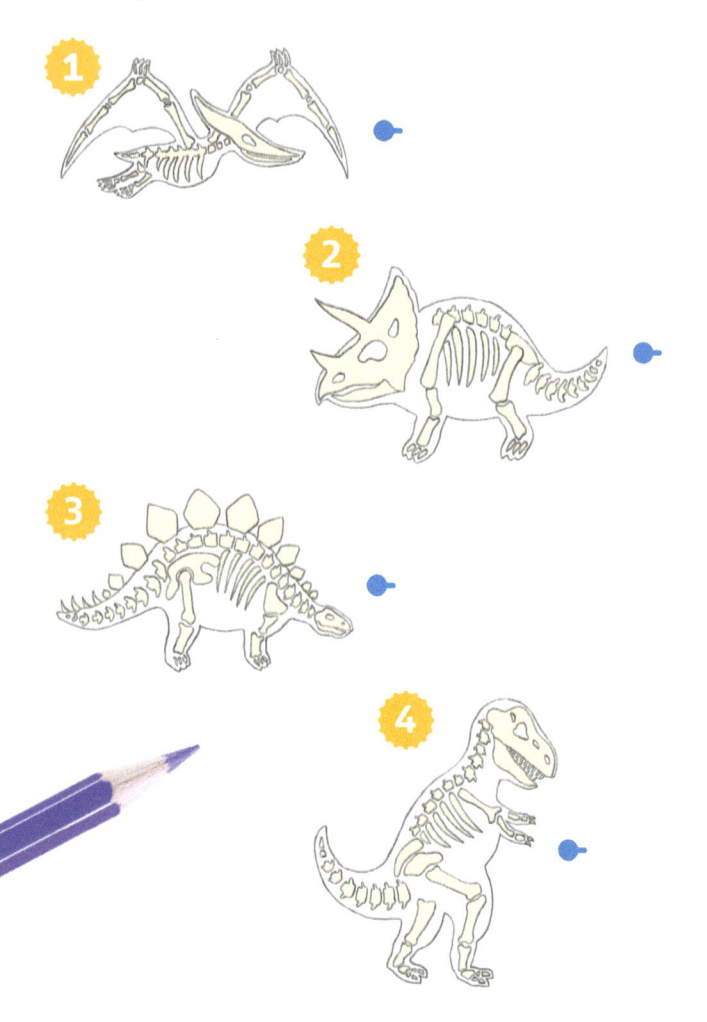

1.
2.
3.
4.

a.
b.
c.
d.

2 WATCH AND CHECK ☑. THEN DESCRIBE FLUFFY'S COSTUME.

46 FORTY-SIX

3 🎧 **LISTEN AND NUMBER. THEN GUESS WITH YOUR PARTNER.**

CODE CRACKER

a b c
d e f

VALUES GIVE SUPPORT.

4 PLAY *SNAP!* SAY *GOOD JOB!* OR *NICE TRY!*

5 💬 **DRAW AND PLAY *GUESS THE PICTURE*.**

PROJECT AND REVIEW

MAKE A DINOSAUR PUZZLE

STEP 1

RESEARCH

- RESEARCH DINOSAURS.
- ☐ WHAT DINOSAURS DO I KNOW?

STEP 2

PLAN

- CHOOSE AND DRAW YOUR DINOSAUR.
- ☐ WHAT DOES MY DINOSAUR LOOK LIKE?

48 FORTY-EIGHT

STEP 3

CREATE

▷ MAKE YOUR DINOSAUR PUZZLE.

☐ WHAT SHAPES CAN I USE?

MAKE A POSTER OF ANIMALS IN DANGER.

STEP 4

SHOW AND TELL

▷ DO A PUZZLE. THEN DESCRIBE THE DINOSAUR.

NOW I CAN ...

... USE DINOSAUR WORDS.

... TALK ABOUT DINOSAURS.

... GIVE SUPPORT AND PRAISE.

FORTY-NINE 49

5 A PICNIC

HOW CAN WE HAVE A PICNIC?

I WILL LEARN PICNIC WORDS.

1 LOOK AT THE PICTURE. WHAT CAN YOU SEE?

2 STICK THE FOOD AND DRINK ON THE PICTURE.

3 LISTEN, POINT, AND REPEAT.

SONG TIME

4 🎧 045 LISTEN AND POINT. THEN SING ALONG AND DANCE.

5 MATCH THE SHAPES. SAY THE FOOD.

MATH ZONE

1. △
2. ○
3. ■
4. ▬
5. ◖

a. (sandwich)
b. (salad)
c. (toast)
d. (orange)
e. (chocolate)

STORY LAB
ENJOYING A STORY

I WILL LISTEN TO A STORY ABOUT A PICNIC.

1 LISTEN TO THE STORY.

PICNIC TIME

VALUES LEARN TO SHARE.

2 DRAW 😃 OR ☹.

3 MAKE PICNIC FOOD FROM CLAY. TALK TO YOUR PARTNER ABOUT LIKES AND DISLIKES.

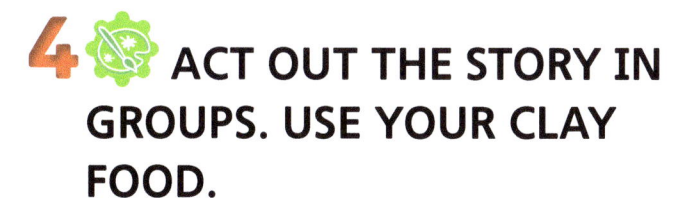

4 ACT OUT THE STORY IN GROUPS. USE YOUR CLAY FOOD.

SOUND LAB
Y AND J

I WILL LEARN THE Y AND J SOUNDS.

1 LISTEN, POINT, AND REPEAT.

2 LISTEN, POINT, AND REPEAT. MATCH THE WORDS THAT START WITH THE SAME SOUND.

3 PLAY *SOUND SOUP*.

4 MAKE A LETTER USING FOOD. SAY THE SOUND.

EXPERIMENT LAB

SCIENCE: QUANTITIES OF SUGAR

I WILL LEARN ABOUT SUGAR.

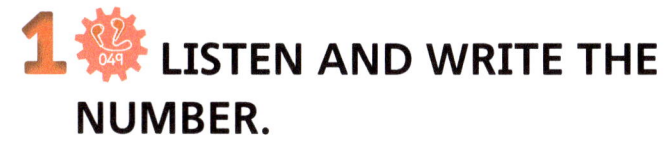

1 LISTEN AND WRITE THE NUMBER.

▶ WATCH A VIDEO ABOUT SUGAR.

2 LOOK AT **1**. COMPLETE THE PICTOGRAPH.

3 HOW MUCH DOES 1 TEASPOON OF SUGAR WEIGH? USE SCALES.

= ☐ G

EXPERIMENT TIME

HOW MANY SPOONS OF SUGAR ARE IN MY FOOD AND DRINK?

2   1   2

FIFTY-FIVE 55

WASH YOUR HANDS!
COMMUNICATION

I WILL GIVE INSTRUCTIONS.

1 🎧 050 **LISTEN AND DRAW 😀 OR ☹. THEN COMPLETE FOR YOU AND SAY.**

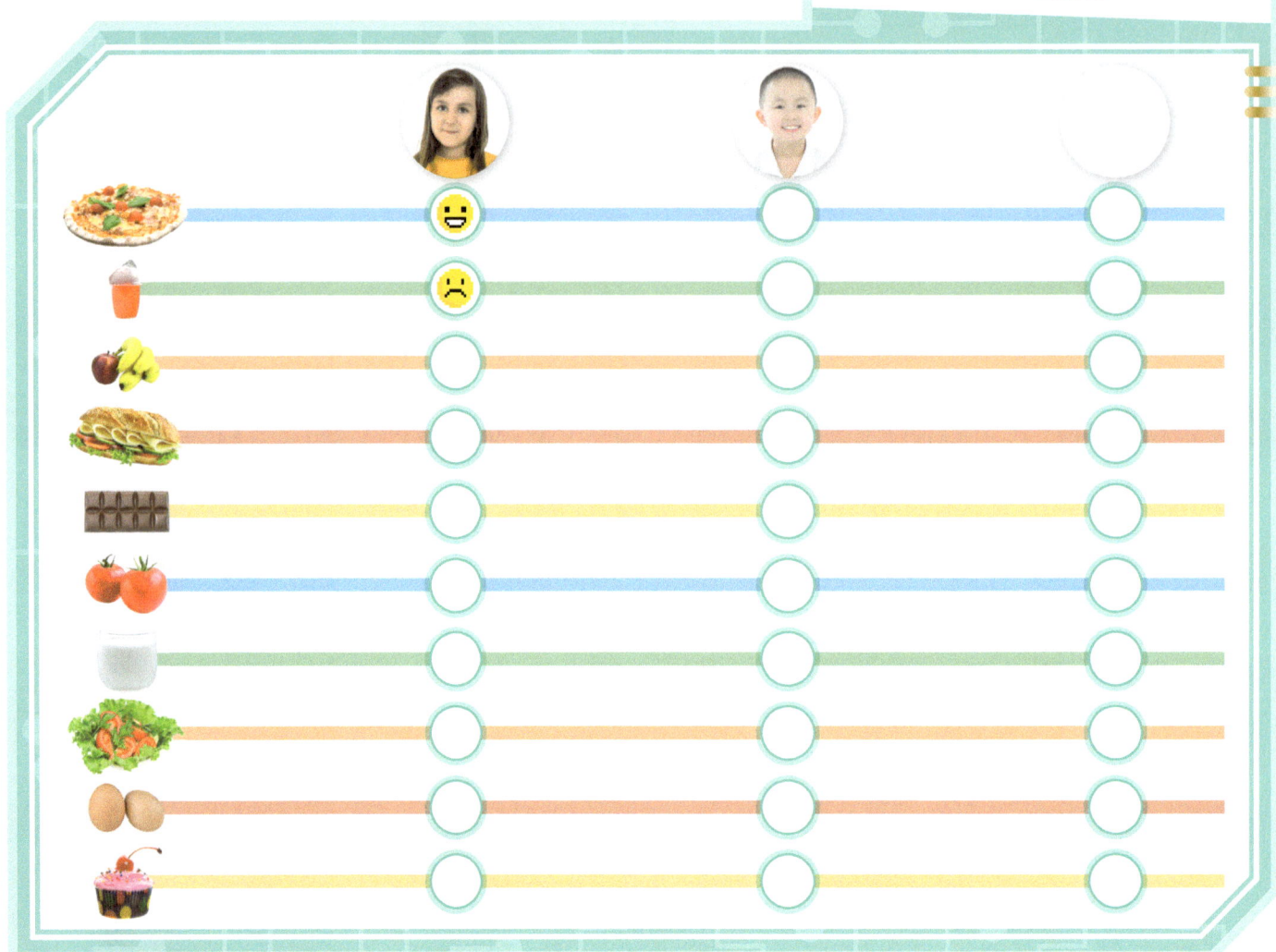

CODE CRACKER

2 ▶ 🎧 051 **WATCH. ORDER AND SAY.**

3 LISTEN AND PLAY *TEDDY SAYS*.

4 LOOK AND CIRCLE. THEN SAY.

CODE CRACKER

5 MAKE RECYCLED SOAP. WASH AND DRY YOUR HANDS.

PROJECT AND REVIEW

HAVE A PICNIC

STEP 1

RESEARCH

RESEARCH FOOD.

☐ WHAT FOOD DO I LIKE?

STEP 2

PLAN

FIND ITEMS YOU NEED FOR THE PICNIC.

☐ WHAT DO I NEED?

STEP 3

CREATE

▶ MAKE YOUR PICNIC.

☐ HOW CAN I SET UP MY PICNIC?

MAKE YOUR OWN PIZZA.

STEP 4

SHOW AND TELL

▶ TALK ABOUT YOUR PICNIC.

NOW I CAN ...

... USE PICNIC WORDS.

... TALK ABOUT PICNICS.

... GIVE INSTRUCTIONS.

FIFTY-NINE 59

6 UNDER THE SEA

HOW CAN I MAKE A DIVING GAME?

I WILL LEARN SEA ANIMAL WORDS.

1 LOOK AT THE PICTURE. WHAT CAN YOU SEE?

2 STICK THE ANIMALS ON THE PICTURE.

3 LISTEN, POINT, AND REPEAT.

SONG TIME

4 LISTEN AND POINT. THEN SING ALONG AND DANCE.

5 COUNT THE ANIMALS IN THE BIG PICTURE. THEN SAY.

MATH ZONE

STORY LAB
ENJOYING A STORY

I WILL LISTEN TO A STORY ABOUT SEA ANIMALS.

1 LISTEN TO THE STORY.

CAN YOU SEE TEETH?

2 CIRCLE THE ANIMALS FROM THE STORY. CHECK WITH YOUR PARTNER.

CODE CRACKER

3 MAKE A FISH TANK. ASK AND ANSWER.

4 ACT OUT THE STORY IN GROUPS. USE YOUR FISH TANK.

SIXTY-THREE 63

SOUND LAB
I AND U

I WILL LEARN THE *I* AND *U* SOUNDS.

1 🔊 056 LISTEN, POINT, AND REPEAT.

2 🔊 057 LISTEN, POINT, AND REPEAT. CIRCLE THE *U* SOUNDS IN BLUE AND THE *I* SOUNDS IN RED.

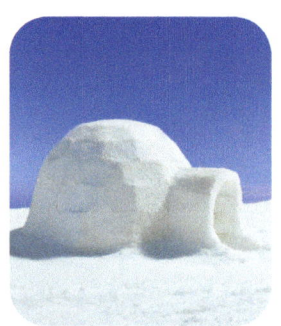

3 💬 PLAY *SOUND FISHING*.

4 🌼 MAKE A LETTER USING SHELLS. SAY THE SOUND.

64 SIXTY-FOUR

EXPERIMENT LAB

SCIENCE: ANIMALS WITH SHELLS

I WILL LEARN ABOUT ANIMALS WITH SHELLS.

1 LISTEN AND CHECK ✓ THE ANIMALS WITH SHELLS.

▶ WATCH A VIDEO ABOUT TURTLES.

2 COLOR THE ANIMALS WITH SHELLS. POINT AND SAY.

3 MAKE A COLLAGE OF SEA AND LAND ANIMALS WITH SHELLS.

EXPERIMENT TIME

CAN I DISSOLVE A SHELL?

SIXTY-FIVE 65

IT'S WINDY!
COMMUNICATION

I WILL TALK ABOUT THE WEATHER.

1 CONTINUE THE SEQUENCE. THEN SAY.

CODE CRACKER

VALUES WEAR SUITABLE CLOTHES.

2 WATCH. DRAW A ☀ OR ☁.

1.

2.

3 LISTEN AND NUMBER. THEN SAY.

4 PLAY *GUESS THE WEATHER*.

5 MAKE A SEASIDE FAN. PLAY *CAN YOU SEE?*

PROJECT AND REVIEW

MAKE A DIVING GAME

STEP 1

RESEARCH

▷ RESEARCH SEA ANIMALS.

☐ WHAT ANIMALS LIVE UNDER THE SEA?

STEP 2

PLAN

▷ FIND ITEMS YOU NEED FOR THE GAME.

☐ WHAT DO I NEED?

68 SIXTY-EIGHT

STEP 3
CREATE

▷ MAKE YOUR GAME.

☐ HOW CAN I DECORATE MY CUP?

STEP 4
SHOW AND TELL

▷ PLAY YOUR GAME.

FIND OUT ABOUT SEA ANIMALS IN COLD PLACES.

NOW I CAN ...

... USE SEA ANIMAL WORDS.

... TALK ABOUT SEA ANIMALS.

... TALK ABOUT THE WEATHER.

SIXTY-NINE 69

CULTURE 2
LUNCH ON THE GO

1 WHAT COLORS CAN YOU SEE IN THE PICTURES? SAY.

2 LISTEN AND POINT.

MY LUNCHBOX

3 DECORATE CHOPSTICKS. PLAY *CHOPSTICK RELAY*.

MY CULTURE

FIND OUT ABOUT LUNCHBOXES IN YOUR COUNTRY.

4 DRAW A LUNCHBOX. THEN DESCRIBE IT TO YOUR PARTNER.

OUR WORLD

INTRO:
HERE WE STAND: CHILDREN OF EVERY AGE,
THIS IS OUR WORLD AND THE WORLD'S OUR STAGE.
WE CAN LAUGH, WE CAN CRY – WE CAN FLOAT, WE CAN FLY,
WE CAN DANCE, WE CAN SING – WE CAN DO ALMOST ANYTHING
IN *OUR* WORLD … OUR *BEAUTIFUL* WORLD.

VERSE 1:
SOME OF US ARE SMALL; SOME OF US ARE TALL,
SOME OF US ARE SHY; SOME SAY HI TO EVERYBODY,
SOME OF US LIKE NUMBERS; SOME OF US LOVE WORDS,
SOME OF US WATCH FOOTBALL, AND SOME OF US WATCH THE BIRDS!

(CHORUS)
THIS IS OUR WORLD … WE'RE DIFFERENT BUT THE SAME.
WE LIVE AND LEARN TOGETHER – WE GET TO KNOW EACH OTHER …
IN *OUR* WORLD … OUR *BEAUTIFUL* WORLD.

VERSE 2:
SOME OF US LIKE MUSIC; SOME OF US LIKE CARS,
SOME OF US DRAW PICTURES, LOOKING AT THE STARS,
SOME OF US ARE SCIENTISTS, TRYING TO FIND THE CODE,
ALL OF US CAN HELP A FRIEND AND GIVE A HAND TO HOLD.

THIS IS OUR WORLD – THERE'S ROOM FOR EVERYONE.
WE LEARN TO LIVE TOGETHER, AND WE HAVE A LOT OF FUN …
IN **OUR** WORLD … IN **OUR** WORLD … IN OUR BEAUTIFUL WORLD!

Aa Bb Cc Dd Ee
Ff Gg Hh Ii Jj
Kk Ll Mm Nn Oo
Pp Qq Rr Ss Tt Uu
Vv Ww Xx Yy Zz

WORDLIST

WELCOME UNIT

FIRST DAY VOCABULARY
BOY
GIRL
GOOD
GOODBYE
HELLO
TEACHER
1–10

UNIT 1

BIRTHDAY PARTY VOCABULARY
BALLOON
BIRTHDAY PARTY
BLUE
CAKE
CARD
GIFT
GREEN
ORANGE
PINK
PURPLE
RED
WHITE
YELLOW

SOUND LAB
BALLOON
BIRTHDAY PARTY
BOY
CAKE
CARD

EXPERIMENT LAB
RAIN
RAINBOW
SUNLIGHT
WATER
WATERFALL

UNIT 2

MUSIC VOCABULARY
DANCE
DRUM
GUITAR
PIANO
SHAKER
SING
TRIANGLE
TRUMPET

SOUND LAB
DANCE
DOG
DOOR
TABLE
TEACHER
TEN

EXPERIMENT LAB
DRUM
EAR
GUITAR
PIANO
SHAKER
SOUND WAVE
TRIANGLE
TRUMPET
XYLOPHONE

UNIT 3

FARM VOCABULARY
BEE
CHICKEN
COW
DUCK
EGG
FOX
SHEEP
TRACTOR

SOUND LAB
ANT
APPLE
FIVE
FOREST
FOUR
FOX

EXPERIMENT LAB
BEES
BUTTER
CHICKENS
COWS
DUCKS
EGGS
HONEY
MILK

CULTURE 1
BEE
CHICKEN
MUSIC
NOISY
PIANO
QUIET
VIOLINS

UNIT 4

DINOSAUR VOCABULARY
DINOSAUR
HORN
LEGS
LIZARD
SPINES
TAIL
TEETH
WINGS

SOUND LAB
EGG
ELBOW
ELEPHANT
LEGS
LIZARD
LUNCH

EXPERIMENT LAB
FLAT TEETH
MEAT
PLANTS
SHARP TEETH

UNIT 5

PICNIC VOCABULARY
CHOCOLATE
FRUIT
MILK
PIZZA
SALAD
SANDWICHES
TOMATOES
YOGURT

WORDLIST

SOUND LAB
JAM
JUG
YELLOW
YO-YO
YOGURT

EXPERIMENT LAB
CAKE
CHOCOLATE
DRINK
FOOD
PIZZA
SPOONS
SUGAR
YOGURT

UNIT 6

UNDER THE SEA VOCABULARY
CRAB
FISH
JELLYFISH
SEAHORSE
SHARK
SHELL
SHRIMP
STARFISH

SOUND LAB
IGLOO
INSECT
INSTRUMENTS
UMBRELLA
UP

EXPERIMENT LAB
CRAB
DISSOLVE
HARD
JELLYFISH
SEAHORSE
SHELL
SHRIMP

CULTURE 2
BENTO BOX
CHOPSTICKS
JAPANESE
LEAF
LUNCHBOX
MEXICAN
SPORK
TAMALE

CONTINENTS
AFRICA
ANTARCTICA
ASIA
AUSTRALIA
EUROPE
NORTH AMERICA
SOUTH AMERICA

English Code

Journey
STARTER

CERTIFICATE

GOOD JOB!

_____
STUDENT'S NAME

_____
TEACHER'S SIGNATURE AND DATE

Pearson

UNIT 2
STORY LAB

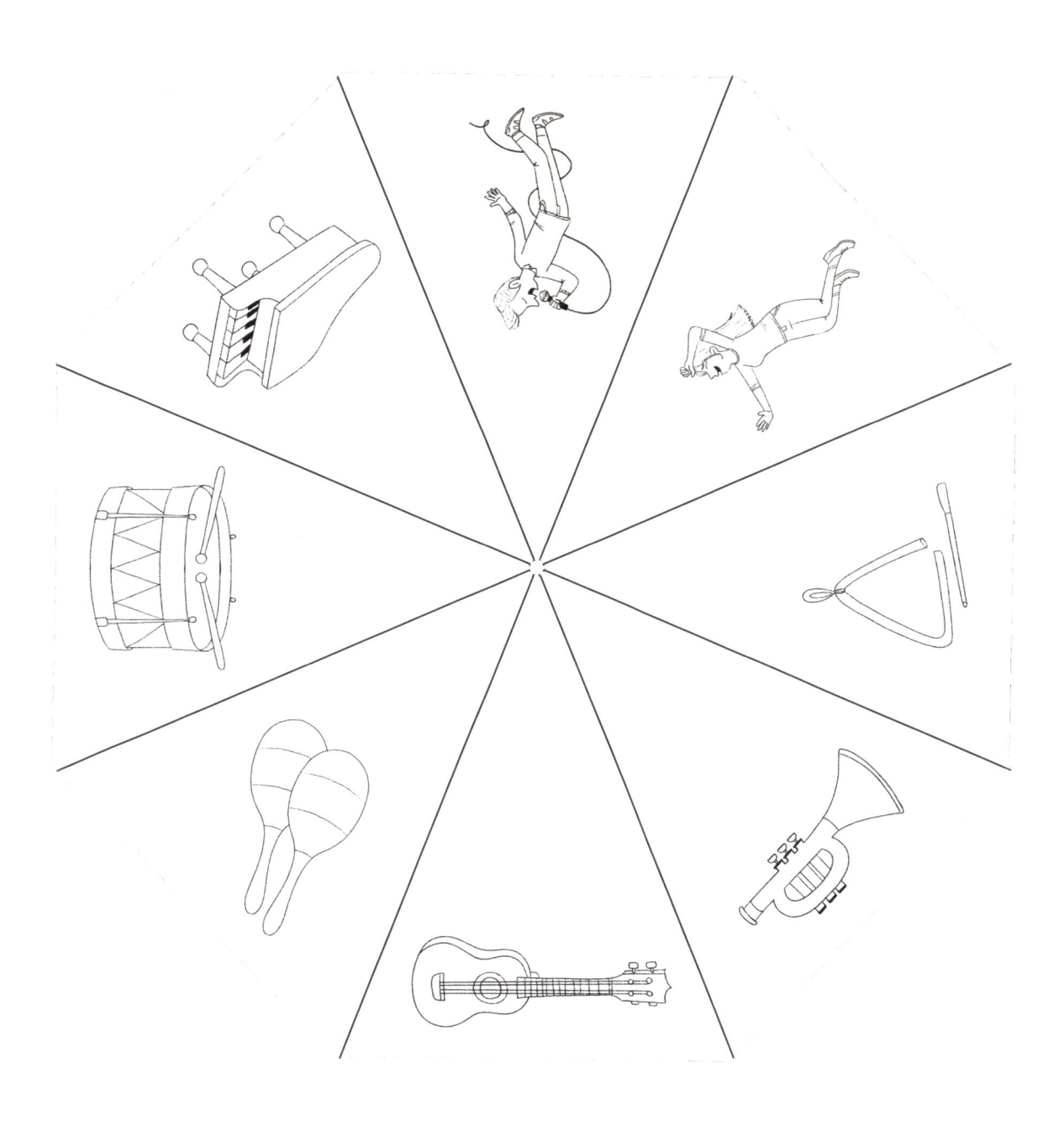

PRESS-OUT

UNIT 3
COMMUNICATION

PRESS-OUT

1. BIRTHDAY FUN!

STICKERS

PAGES 8–9

2. MUSIC TIME!

PAGES 18–19

3. AT THE FARM

PAGES 28-29

4. MY DINOSAUR

PAGES 40–41

5. A PICNIC

PAGES 50–51

6. UNDER THE SEA

PAGES 60–61

STICKERS

NOW I CAN ...

STICKERS